BUILDING BLOCKS TO SELF-ESTEEM

I Like Who I Am & It Shows

STRATEGIES FOR ENHANCING SELF-ESTEEM

by Barbara Valdez

Fearon Teacher Aids
A Paramount Communications Company

Editorial Director: Virginia L. Murphy
Editors: Marilyn Trow and Sue Mogard
Copyeditor: Lisa Schwimmer
Book Design: Teena Remer
Cover Design and Illustration: Lucyna Green
Inside Illustration: Lucyna Green

Credit:
Children at Risk Information on Pages 4-5
Text excerpt, pp. 43-44 from THE MAGIC OF ENCOURAGEMENT
by Stephanie Marston. Text Copyright © 1990 by Stephanie Marston.
By permission of William Morrow & Company, Inc.

ISBN 0-86653-952-2

Printed in the United States of America

1. 9 8 7 6 5 4 3 2

Contents

Introduction

A book alone cannot provide healthy self-esteem in young children. Only love, understanding, and attention can help children improve their concepts of themselves. This resource is a guide to help you, the teacher, improve children's self-esteem in the classroom. The rest is up to the children's families and even the children themselves.

Why Enhance Self-Esteem?

Self-esteem is defined by Webster's dictionary as self-respect or a strong belief in oneself. Children often develop self-destructive behaviors when they lack a positive sense of self. It is vitally important for schools to take a part in enhancing children's self-esteem. If children are to develop high self-esteem and become happy, fulfilled adults, we as educators must help children (1) see themselves as valued members of a group, possessing unique qualities; (2) feel comfortable expressing themselves with others; and (3) learn the skills to maintain a sense of personal control over their lives. Children possessing these building blocks to self-esteem are better able to cope with life's stresses and have the tools to continue to grow throughout their lives. As adults, these children will tend to make better life choices.

Children at Risk

Many of the children's social problems can be reduced by improving children's self-esteem. Children who lack good self-esteem are "at risk." This implies that when we speak of building self-esteem, we identify not only those children in our classrooms with the obvious problems— poor home environments (or no home environment at all), drugs, learning disabilities, and so on—but also the children who skip breakfast, are over-achievers and feel pressure to always be perfect, and other seemingly "good" children as well.

Children at risk exhibit the characteristics of children with low self-esteem. Consider the following information from *Magic of Encouragement* by Stephanie Marston. New York: William Morrow and Company, 1990.

A child with high self-esteem:

- ❤ is proud of his or her accomplishments.
- ❤ can act independently.
- ❤ assumes responsibility.
- ❤ can tolerate frustration.
- ❤ approaches challenges with enthusiasm.

♥ feels capable of taking charge of situations in his or her own life.

♥ has a good sense of humor.

♥ has a sense of purpose.

♥ can postpone gratification.

♥ seeks help when needed.

♥ is confident and resourceful.

♥ is active, energetic, and spontaneously expresses his or her feelings.

♥ is relaxed and can manage stress.

Whereas,

A child with low self-esteem:

♥ plays it safe by avoiding situations that require taking risks.

♥ feels powerless.

♥ becomes easily frustrated.

♥ is overly sensitive.

♥ constantly needs reassurance.

♥ is easily influenced by others.

♥ frequently uses the phrases "I don't know" or "I don't care."

♥ is withdrawn.

♥ blames others for his [or her] failures.

♥ is isolated, has few friends, is preoccupied.

♥ is uncooperative, angry.

♥ is uncommunicative.

♥ is clingy, dependent.

♥ is constantly complaining.

♥ has a general negative attitude.

Promoting Self-Esteem in the Classroom

As children, many of us had mentors or encouragement from an adult that made a difference in our lives. Providing children with positive school experiences is one way to stop destructive behaviors and help children realize their worth as human beings. We as teachers do and can make a difference in how children perceive themselves. Helping children feel good about themselves is perhaps the most valuable asset we can instill in children. The strategies in the *Building Blocks to Self-Esteem* series provide marvelous avenues for you to explore with children that can lead to a sense of higher self-esteem.

Begin with the basics. Make your classroom into a diverse environment. Make sure art materials available in your classroom are in a wide range of colors—multiracial. Provide all skin colors—tan, brown, red, beige, and so on—in your paint and paper materials. Provide different skin-tone colors of crayon as well. In the dramatic-play area and among the manipulatives—puzzles and games—make sure that different races are represented.

Be aware of the pictures you display in the classroom. Are all races represented? Are there as many pictures of boys as there are of girls? Do you choose holiday pictures that represent many beliefs and cultures?

Keep in mind that most children need quiet or "alone" time, too. When children begin to feel pressured and too many details lead to stressful situations, it may help to play some soft music. Have quiet music available so that children can slow down and not feel pressured.

Children need to know that what is important is not what they do or accomplish, but who they are.

A Personal Look at Self-Esteem

The quality of our relationships with children will depend upon our own level or degree of self-esteem. Teachers need to take responsibility for their own positive self-worth. Our effectiveness as teachers is influenced by how we feel about ourselves. Teachers who have well-developed communication skills succeed in establishing, maintaining, and promoting good relationships in the classroom. These teachers often have open communication and support in their classrooms that help promote high self-esteem in children.

It should be expected that any new methods you may try from this book may at first seem unfamiliar. Accept this as a natural process. Practice slowly. Focus on the feelings of the children. Help children focus on their feelings as well. Then listen, listen, listen! There is no better time to help children realize their full potential for success than now.

At the beginning of each lesson, take a minute to think about how you feel about each self-esteem issue. Then examine what you've done in the past, as well as what you see now as the best way to promote positive self-esteem in your classroom. Use the Reflection pages provided at the end of each section to assess your classroom efforts at building a more positive self-esteem in the children.

Self-Esteem and the Home

One of the most important aspects of helping children with their self-esteem is to work in tandem with the home. Parents, guardians, and families play a vital role in a child's feelings of self-worth. This cannot be stressed enough. Keep the lines of communication open with parents or guardians.

A letter to parents may be helpful in setting up positive communication between you and the parents or guardians of your students. Use the letter on page 8 to introduce this unit to parents and guardians and open the door for their participation.

Special Self-Esteem Issues

Some children are at risk because of unhealthy home environments—drug abuse, alcoholism, sexual abuse, verbal abuse, and so on. Children sometimes get teased because their parents are receiving welfare aid as well. We, as teachers, may not be social workers, but we do need to be aware of these situations and know what we can do to help these children.

The children in these homes need lots of attention. Without labeling the children, try to give these individual children the attention and structure that they need. Children need to know the classroom is a safe place for them to be.

Children from unhealthy home environments need a warm and strong relationship with the adults in the classroom. Reassure these children often of their worth by giving them honest, special attention—pats on the back, so to speak, without overdoing it to the detriment of the other children in the classroom.

Dear Parent,

As your child's teacher, I am working to help your child realize his or her full potential. Throughout the year, I will be initiating projects and activities that will help promote healthy self-esteem. Some of these projects, events, and activities include you and your family and I will periodically be asking for your help.

I've included with this letter some ways you can start helping your child every day. Though these ideas are not new, I would like to share them with you.

❏ **Read to your child each day.**

If you would rather not read, or feel uncomfortable reading, tell your child stories—either ones you know by heart or stories about when you were a child. Sharing a book is an expression of love.

❏ **Make sure your child has a good night's sleep.**

This helps your child concentrate better at school.

❏ **Make sure your child has something to eat before coming to school.**

According to nutritionists, breakfast is the most important meal of the day.

❏ **Accept your child as he or she is.**

Accept the uniqueness of your child. Praise your child's positive actions, feelings, and ideas.

❏ **A child needs to learn how to be helpful and to have structure in his or her life.**

A child should be assigned simple chores each day. Some beginning chores can be to sweep the floor, help make the bed, fold clothing, or take out the garbage. Success with small tasks helps give children confidence.

❏ **Each child and adult needs a quiet place.**

There are times when a child has to study for school or needs a place just to be alone with him or herself. A quiet place doesn't have to be fancy. It can be a corner of a room or a space on a porch or a stair landing.

❏ **Make your child an active member of your household.**

Children will grow and develop when they know they have a role in the household and that their role is respected. Children should feel free to express their opinions without fear of ridicule.

❏ **Tell your child each day that you love him or her.**

Expressing love does wonders!

As the year progresses, your child will bring home journal pages showing what we've been studying in school. Ask your child to explain his or her drawings—and give lots of praise and interest.

Thank you for your cooperation.

Sincerely,

I Like Who I Am & It Shows © 1993 Fearon Teacher Aids

I Am Unique

Children learn to respect themselves when we help them see how special they are. When children are encouraged to see how special their characteristics and personalities are, their creativity and learning abilities greatly improve.

Building Blocks Strategies Included in This Unit

- ❤ Accepting Physical Characteristics
- ❤ Affirming Strengths and Needs
- ❤ Appreciating Comparisons
- ❤ Enjoying Celebrations
- ❤ Exploring Learning Styles
- ❤ Expressing Myself
- ❤ Recognizing My Own Worthiness

Accepting Physical Characteristics

Take a Minute...

Children accept physical differences in others when they have a positive sense of their own physical selves. Most of us remember children singled out by others for being different, whether heavy, thin, wearing glasses, or using a wheelchair. Give the children an opportunity to talk to others about these differences. Consider these options:

- Invite a person who uses a wheelchair to come in and explain how a wheelchair works and why he or she uses one. Encourage children to ask questions. Learning in a safe environment about wheelchairs and why they are used will help children understand that wheelchairs and their users are not "strange" or "frightening."

- Invite several children and adults who wear glasses or hearing aids to the classroom to talk to the children. Encourage questions from the children.

Strategies to Focus on Self-Esteem

Talk About Growing with the Children

Each child grows at his or her own unique rate. Helping children understand changes in their bodies will give them a sense of well-being. Discuss the positive growth changes children have experienced since they were babies. Since children have many feelings about the changes in their bodies that they experience each year, it is best to focus on individual growth changes and avoid making comparisons between children. Invite children to draw pictures of themselves when they were babies and then pictures of themselves now (see journal page on 12).

"How has your body changed since you were a baby?"

"Are these changes helpful? Why or why not?"

Encourage Children to Discover the Limits of Their Bodies

Enjoying physical activities helps children feel at ease with their physical selves. Invite the children to demonstrate or tell about things they are able to do with their bodies, such as jump, run, turn cartwheels, and so on. Encourage children to appreciate the many different things everyone in the classroom can do!

"Does everyone like doing the same movements with their bodies? Why or why not?"

"What is your favorite way to move your body? Why?"

Invite Children to Accept Different Sizes of Others

Not everyone is the same size, shape, or weight. Children can learn to appreciate the diversity of our physical shapes. Set up a bulletin board in the classroom entitled "Famous People." Children can collect pictures of people whom they like—showing that these people come in various sizes, shapes, and races.

Encourage Children to Compare Hands and Feet

Invite the children to notice how many different sizes of people are in the classroom! Place tempera paint in a large cake pan. Add liquid detergent to help with clean-up. Have a "foot day" and invite children to take off their shoes and socks. Then have each child step into the paint and then onto butcher paper one foot at a time. Have a "hand day" as well. After the paint is dry, children can compare their handprints or footprints. How many are alike? How many are different? Do this activity with a parent volunteer or a student helper. Have a pan of soapy water nearby for cleanup.

Help Children Notice Everyday Differences

Make a "Hair Chart" for the classroom. Invite the children to see the differences in hair color among the children. Eye color can be charted in a similar way. Then discuss the differences.

Hair Color
Brown
Black
Red
Blonde

Talk About Differences Openly

Discuss with the children why some people need glasses. Explain some of the reasons for wearing glasses. Then have children collect pictures from magazines of famous people who wear glasses. You may want to ask an ophthalmologist to come to your classroom and talk to the children about glasses and why people wear them. Do this same activity with people who wear braces, use walkers, use wheelchairs, and so on.

Emphasize Uniqueness

Encourage children to think about what is unique about themselves. Talk about how each of us has special characteristics that, when put all together, make a unique person! Then invite children to draw pictures of themselves that show how unique they are (see journal page on page 13).

Name _____

Look How I Have Changed!

I Like Who I Am & It Shows © 1993 Fearon Teacher Aids

Name _____

I Am Unique!

Affirming Strengths and Needs

Take a Minute...

When children realize that it is okay to ask for help and that their accomplishments, however small, are important, they feel good about themselves. Consider these options:

- Talk about families. Ask the children what their families say they do well at home.

- Share with the children things that you do well. Tell them about a time when someone helped you and how good you felt.

Strategies to Focus on Self-Esteem

Encourage Children to Focus on Their Accomplishments

Children need to know that they are able to do many things well. Helping children delight in their own abilities adds to their overall sense of well-being. Ask children to share things that they do well, such as riding a bike, singing a song, and so on. Then help each child make a poster of what he or she can do well using the journal page on page 15. Make a poster of your own strengths as well. Tape the posters on large sheets of construction paper to make frames. Display the posters in the classroom. Then invite parents and visitors to the classroom to share in the display. Encourage children and guests to add compliments to the posters. Point out that everyone has special strengths to enjoy and share with others.

"How do you feel when you are able to do something well?"

"Can everyone do the same things? Why or why not?"

Help Children Identify Their Needs and Accept Needs As a Normal Part of Life

Encouraging children to express their needs helps children feel okay about themselves. When children learn acceptable ways to state their needs, they are better able to see life as a process of growth and not become too discouraged by little setbacks. Invite the children to think about something they might like to be able to do better. Share some of your own needs with the children as well. Point out that everyone has needs, even though the needs may be different. Brainstorm ways that children might ask for help when they need something. Then invite the children to draw pictures of things they want to learn to do better (see journal page on page 16). Draw a picture of yourself as well!

"How can you get help to learn to do something better?"

Name _____

Look What I Do Well!

Name _____

I Want To Do This Better!

I Like Who I Am & It Shows © 1993 Fearon Teacher Aids

Appreciating Comparisons

Take a Minute...

Children relate well to others when they recognize their own interests and abilities. Comparing one child with another can be destructive. Build self-esteem by helping children appreciate their own abilities, interests, and ideas. Think about the uniqueness of each child in your classroom. If someone admires something that one child has done, and another child has done as well in another area, point out to both children that each has certain capabilities—one child is good at one thing, someone else is good at another, but everyone is trying to do his or her best. Consider these options:

- The child who is having problems in some academic area may shine in other areas. Ask that child to be a peer tutor in his or her area of strength. Someone else in the class may be peer-tutoring in the weak area of that child. The child who can tie shoelaces, for example, is sometimes a better teacher of shoelace-tying than the adult who looks at it from an adult point of view.

- Every child can become an expert at some skill outside the classroom. Take advantage of this "expertness." This helps to develop positive feelings in the children. Children can share their knowledge about how to make toast, fold a paper airplane, use a hammer, and so on.

Strategies to Focus on Self-Esteem

Invite Children to Talk About the Special Things They Each Can Do

Children need to feel they are able to do some things that are uniquely special to them. When children are able to value the fact that no one else can show affection for their pets, sing for their grandparents, or tell a story at the supper table to their families the way they do, they see themselves as uniquely valued. Help children identify the special things they bring to their families, friends, and the classroom. Then invite children to draw pictures of something special only they can do (see journal page on page 19).

"Name something only you are able to do with your family."

"Are any two people exactly alike? Why or why not?"

Discuss the Unique Ways That a Task May Be Done

How children complete daily tasks makes them special. When children are valued for the individual ways they complete daily tasks, they come to see themselves as special and unique! Invite the children to share how they brush their teeth, make sandwiches, draw pictures, and so on (see journal page on page 20). Encourage the children to see that there are many different ways to accomplish the same task.

"How do you get ready for school in the morning?"

"How many ways are there to count the blocks? Try it and see! Can you discover more ways?"

Name _____

I Can!

Name _____

There Are Many Different Ways To Do Things!

I Like Who I Am & It Shows © 1993 Fearon Teacher Aids

Enjoying Celebrations

Take a Minute...

Children learn to value themselves when they can share special celebrations in their homes and focus on their uniqueness. Every family has a special way of celebrating, whether it is in a traditional or unusual sense. Think about special celebrations and how they relate to each of the children. Be aware of religious and cultural differences in your classroom. Consider these options:

- Talk about different winter celebrations besides Christmas, such as Hanukkah and Kwanzaa.

- Invite children to celebrate holidays that they are not familiar with—the Chinese New Year, Japanese Children's Day, and so on.

Strategies to Focus on Self-Esteem

Encourage Self-Esteem by Acknowledging Special Family Celebrations

Children like to feel that they are special. Sharing about unique family celebrations will help them appreciate their specialness. Make a class list of the many ways children celebrate with their families. Ask the children to share the celebrations that they like most. Discuss ways the children learn about themselves through their family celebrations. Then invite the children to draw pictures of their favorite celebrations with their families on the journal page on page 23.

"What are some family celebrations that you enjoy? Tell us about them."

"Why are these celebrations important to you?"

Discuss the Significance of Celebrating Individual Birthdays

Children like to be personally celebrated. Celebrating birthdays in the classroom is an especially fun way for all young children to learn to see themselves as valuable to others. Invite children to share how they feel about growing older and experiencing birthdays. Encourage children to discuss the feelings they have at their birthday celebrations and other enjoyable birthday celebrations they have attended. Ask children to draw a picture of themselves on their birthdays (see journal page on page 24)!

"Do you enjoy your birthday celebrations? Do you like going to your friends' birthday celebrations?"

"What is your favorite part of a birthday celebration?"

Discuss Different Holidays Celebrations

There are many children who do not celebrate the holidays that are customarily celebrated, such as Christmas or Easter. Help the children understand these differences among children. Discuss the holidays children celebrate during the year. List each of these on a large class calendar. Recognize the holidays and the children who celebrate them as each day approaches. Keep in mind that Jewish children, Jehovah Witnesses, and Southeast Asian children may feel left out during Christian holidays.

Share Holiday Traditions

Children might want to share music, records, or songs that are a part of a family custom or tradition. There are many children from a variety of countries that are now students in our schools. Take this opportunity to inform all children of our country's wonderful diversity. Be sure to include discussions about the different foods, cooking utensils, and other items used for holiday celebrations of all kinds. Are certain foods eaten at different holidays? Do families use a variety of cooking utensils for these foods? Talk about these issues and help children become aware of cultural differences.

Name _____

I Celebrate With My Family!

Name _____

This Is Me On My Birthday!

Exploring Learning Styles

Take a Minute...

Children learn at different levels and paces. Think about the variety of learning styles in your classroom. What does each child need? What can you do to help each child feel comfortable with his or her own learning style? Consider these options:

- If at all possible, find the time to talk to each child about what he or she is doing and see what learning method he or she is most comfortable with.

- When necessary, give children special space at different times to do tasks, learn something new, or just play.

- Be aware of frustration levels.

Strategies to Focus on Self-Esteem

Offer a Variety of Settings for Learning

It is important for children to discover their learning styles so they can achieve their best in the classroom. Arrange classroom furniture and materials to provide many different individual and group work areas. Then invite the children to choose their own working areas for completing assigned tasks or exploring materials. Invite children to use the journal page on page 26 to draw pictures of their best place to work.

"Which work area will you choose when you are looking at a book? Drawing a picture? Working a puzzle?"

"What is you favorite work area? Why?"

Invite Children to Create Special Work Areas in the Classroom

Inviting children to help make their classroom environment a better place to learn helps children realize that their ideas and needs are valued. Encourage children to help plan new work areas for the classroom. A large refrigerator box or a decorated sheet draped over a table makes a great individualized work area! As a class, decide what types of work areas are needed. Establish rules for each area as well.

"What work areas would be helpful to add to our classroom?"

Encourage Children's Opinions and Feelings

Asking children their opinions or feelings about things gives children a sense of being valued. Help children complete the journal page on page 27 and talk about their responses. Be sure to help children with the words.

Name _____

My Best Place To Work!

Name _____

Look How I Learn!

Circle your favorite way to learn each subject.

 reading

 Quiet   Music   Alone   With Others

 math

 Quiet   Music   Alone   With Others

 **drawing**

 Quiet   Music   Alone   With Others

 **thinking**

 Quiet   Music   Alone    With Others

I Like Who I Am & It Shows © 1993 Fearon Teacher Aids

Expressing Myself

Take a Minute...

Children value their uniqueness when they are encouraged to express their ideas and feelings. Ask children often how they feel about things. Listen to their ideas. It is possible that the children are unable to express themselves anywhere else but in the classroom. Think about how each child expresses him or herself. Stay open to new ideas. When ideas and feelings are accepted and valued, children learn to value themselves. Consider these options:

- Ask for the children's opinions when changing something in the classroom. Ask for new ideas as well.

- Look for suppressed feelings. Let children know that it's okay to express their feelings in healthy ways.

Strategies to Focus on Self-Esteem

Show Children That Their Feelings and Ideas Are Valued

When children are constantly being told what to think and do, they cease to value their own ideas and preferences. Ask children to show their preferences about a series of statements by putting thumbs up for "I agree" and thumbs down for "I disagree." Stop periodically to ask children to share their ideas about a statement. Help the children understand that everyone has different ways of "seeing" each idea presented. Some possible statements include:

"I like going to the grocery store."

"I like cleaning my room."

"I like to play soccer."

"I like reading stories."

"I like eating broccoli."

Invite children to draw pictures of their feelings and ideas. Use the journal page on page 30.

Encourage Children to Freely Explore Their Ideas

Children thrive in activities where they are free to openly express themselves. Children see uniqueness in their own self-expression. Provide a wide variety of art materials that the children may use daily in a designated work area. Display the children's creations in the classroom. Schedule time for children to share their artwork. Then invite children to come up with a new invention. Ask the children to draw pictures of their new inventions using the journal page on page 31.

"What new materials would you like to have in the art center this week?"

"What might you make using buttons, string, and straws?"

Name _____

These Things Make Me Feel Like This...

I Like Who I Am & It Shows © 1993 Fearon Teacher Aids

Name _____

My Invention!

Recognizing My Own Worthiness

Take a Minute...

Children treat others with respect and kindness when they see themselves as capable and lovable. Because of low self-esteem, children sometimes make up stories—possibly to make themselves feel important or because they are fearful of the consequences of a wrongdoing. If children are treated with respect and kindness, they tend to return the same behavior. Think about the actions of the children in your classroom. How can you help those who cannot see their own value? Responsibilities in class can help a child realize his or her worth to the classroom. Consider these options:

- Give out tasks freely—not as punishment, but as responsibilities—tasks that you want only specific children to do, such as paper passer, light-switch monitor, putting away blocks, and so on. Help children feel good about themselves by having each child be a participant in a classroom responsibility.

- Be sure helper roles in the classroom are not dependent upon "good" behavior. Children learn best by example. When assigning special jobs, use an alphabetical system or draw names out of a box.

- Discuss the classroom set-up with parents and guardians and suggest that they might want to help children exercise self-discipline and responsibility at home as well. Encourage parents to give their children special responsibilities in the home. Some ideas are:

  - ❤ straighten up their bed each day

  - ❤ remembering their lunch box

  - ❤ hanging up or folding clothes and putting them in the proper place

  - ❤ putting soiled clothing in the proper place

  - ❤ simple mealtime tasks, such as putting silverware on the table, clearing the table, drying dishes, and so on

  - ❤ dusting the rungs of chairs, the legs of tables

  - ❤ wiping up spills on the floor

Strategies to Focus on Self-Esteem

Help Children See That They Are All Valued

When children feel valued, they will be capable of valuing others. Encourage children to share positive things about themselves—as family members, classroom helpers, playmates on the playground, and so on. Reaffirm how each child's individual interests and abilities are helpful and needed by others. Invite the children to use the journal page on page 34 to draw pictures of what a good friend or family member he or she is!

Child: "I feed the dog every day."

Teacher: "That's very responsible!"

Provide Time for Children to Share About Themselves

It is important for children to share about themselves with others. It is also important for others to recognize and respond to what each child is sharing. Set up a classroom schedule when children may talk about themselves with the class and share special items brought from home. Send a letter home to parents or guardians asking them to help by sending snapshots, stories, or remembrances to school (see page 35). Encourage the class to listen carefully as each child speaks and ask questions, if they wish. Then ask the children to give each speaker a standing ovation to make the speaker feel important and valued by his or her classmates. Display the shared items in the classroom. Then help each child complete the journal page on page 36. Invite children to draw pictures of one of their favorite things!

"What is your favorite color? Pet? Food? Song?"

"What do you like to do at home?"

Consider Those Who Feel Left Out

Sometimes children feel left out because they do not have the same material things or experiences that other members of the class may have. An assignment that is given in class could cause some of the children to feel like outsiders because they can't talk or write about the assignment as presented. When children have an assignment to write or talk about pets, for example, ask those children without pets to write or tell about a pet they would like to have. If talking about vacations, ask children to tell about a special vacation they would like to go on with their families.

Involve Children in Keeping the Classroom Organized

Help children be responsible for straightening up books, picking up toys and scraps from the floor, and making sure the closet or clothes hooks are in order. Involve everyone in this activity—this makes it fun as well as a learning experience.

Name _____

I Am A Good Friend!

I Like Who I Am & It Shows © 1993 Fearon Teacher Aids

Dear _____,

Next week your child is being honored as Child of the Week in our classroom. We would like to have you share that experience with us by asking if you would send to school a snapshot, picture, or other remembrance of your child's younger days. We will display these items on our bulletin board and return them to you after the week is over.

Thank you.

Sincerely,

Name _____

I Want To Tell You About Me!

This is one of my favorite things.

I Like Who I Am & It Shows © 1993 Fearon Teacher Aids

Reflections:

How I Encourage Uniqueness in My Classroom

❑ I plan special celebrations with the children.

❑ I provide time for children to share about family celebrations.

❑ I introduce children to cultural holidays they may not be familiar with.

❑ I offer children opportunities to complete tasks in their own ways.

❑ I encourage children to talk about their interests and abilities.

❑ I invite children to share their feelings about physical growth changes.

❑ I encourage children to do a variety of physical activities and gain confidence with their body movements.

❑ I invite children to see and accept differences in people around them.

❑ I give children the opportunity to talk about differences, such as people who use wheelchairs, wear glasses, and so on.

❑ I enlist the children's help in classroom planning, such as choosing snacks, songs, books, and so on.

❑ I offer a wide variety of art materials for children to use to express themselves imaginatively. These materials are available every day!

❑ I encourage children to share their abilities with others and to ask for help when needed.

❑ I offer the children opportunities to help one another by peer-tutoring or sharing experience.

❑ I offer children a wide variety of work areas for completing tasks.

❑ I invite children to share about themselves.

❑ I help children recognize their personal value through helping in the classroom, being a good friend, and sharing ways they are important to their families.

I Am Connected

Children need to establish strong connections to the important people in their lives and feel that there are special things that belong just to them.
Children also need to see that there is a special place in the world for them before they can successfully relate to others.

Building Blocks Strategies Included in This Unit

- ❤ Belonging to a Family
- ❤ Building Trust
- ❤ Celebrating Diversity
- ❤ Contributing to a Group
- ❤ Coping with Loss
- ❤ Learning to Communicate

Belonging to a Family

Take a Minute...

A good relationship with one's family plays an important part in a child's positive self-image. Children will have more confidence in relationships with others when they see themselves as vital parts of their families. When children see themselves as loved and important, they are able to build good relationships outside of their homes. Be sensitive to each child's unique family situation. A family may be a mother and child, a father and a brother, or a foster family—what each child has is his or her own unique family unit. Remember, the family and self-esteem are intertwined. Consider these options:

- Talk about families and different family situations often in the classroom. This leaves room for discussion and children know their family situations, even if different, are okay.

- Include the families in class activities as often as possible—even if you are just letting the families of the children know what activities and events are going on in the classroom.

Strategies to Focus on Self-Esteem

Discuss the Special Role Each Child Plays in His or Her Family

Children who feel they are important to their families see themselves as safe and cared for and have a sense of well-being. Invite children to share what they enjoy doing with their families and how they contribute to family life. Help children see value in being a helping family member. Encourage children to take pride in doing special household jobs, such as taking out the garbage, setting the table, cleaning their rooms, and so on. Children may enjoy acting out family activities for their classmates. Then invite children to draw pictures of themselves with their families (see journal page on page 42).

"How are you important to your family?"

"What special jobs do you have in your home?"

Share Picturebooks About Family Life

When children see that they belong to a family that cares about one another, they feel more confident in relating to others outside the family unit. Point out that there are many different kinds of families. Provide reading material that depicts a variety of different types of families, such as single-parent, guardians or foster parents, extended families living together, and two-parent families. Books with animal families are great resources as well. Two books are listed here for your convenience.

My Mama Needs Me by Mildred Putts Walter. New York: Lothrop, Lee & Shepard Books, 1983.

The Berenstain Bears Get in a Fight by Jan and Stan Berenstain. New York: Random House, 1988.

Talk to the Children About How They Can Express Emotions

Ask the children how they would tell a family member that they love them. Tell the children that though they may not like what a person is doing, they can still love that person. Explain that even if someone who loves them doesn't like something that they do, that person can still love them. Keep in mind that parents may have problems with expressing love to children because they themselves may lack self-esteem or have trouble expressing their feelings. During a parent meeting or conference or at an open house, talk about these issues and discuss the fact that families are crucial to nurturing a child's self-esteem.

Name _____

My
Family

my mom

my Dog
Sam

my Sister

I Like Who I Am & It Shows © 1993 Fearon Teacher Aids

Building Trust

Take a Minute...

Trust is a delicate subject. Children are able to trust others when they feel secure in their environment. One of the keys to a sense of security and trust is for adults, including the children's teacher, to be consistent with discipline, direction, and promises. Children are quick to pick up on inconsistencies that lead to a lack of security. Think about the trust you convey to the children in your classroom. Consider these options:

- Explain to the children that to trust someone means someone will do what they say they are going to do.

- Talk about trust openly in the classroom. Ask each child who they trust the most. Ask them why they trust that person.

Strategies to Focus on Self-Esteem

Talk About the Important People in Children's Lives

Children need to feel safe and respected by those who care about them if they are to gain a sense of trust in others. Identifying people who they can trust helps children feel safe. Encourage children to suggest names of people whom they might ask for help on the playground, in the classroom, at home, and so on. Ask the children to give reasons for their choices. Reinforce that it is okay for a child not to trust someone if that person makes the child feel uncomfortable. Invite children to draw pictures of someone they trust (see journal page on page 45).

"How does someone show that they care for you?"

"When might you not want to ask someone for help?"

Show Children That You Are Trustworthy

It is important to help children know that their needs are important to you. When you listen to children, you show that you care about their needs and feelings. Children will grow to trust you. Encourage children to express their needs. Then listen, listen, listen! Avoid judgments. You don't need to help children solve their problems—unless the children ask for your help. Invite children to express their worries to you. Ask what they worry about. Encourage children to draw pictures of the things they worry about most (see journal page on page 46). Be sure to discuss the pictures as well.

Talk About Trust in the Children Themselves

As the children determine what they can trust about other people, it is a good opportunity to help them understand that other people have to be able to trust them as well. Ask children to name some things that their families and friends can trust them to do. Help children express their ideas in pictures using the journal page on page 47.

Name _____

Look Who Cares About Me!

Name _____

I Worry About...

I Like Who I Am & It Shows © 1993 Fearon Teacher Aids

Name _____

I Can Be Trusted To...

Celebrating Diversity

Take a Minute...

Today there are many different cultures represented in our country and in our classrooms. When children are proud of their own cultural and ethnic backgrounds, and that pride is celebrated by others as well, children appreciate other cultures and backgrounds as well. Think about the different cultures and ethnic backgrounds present in your classroom. Consider these options:

- Celebrate special holidays that may be new to children, such as Kwanzaa, Japanese Children's Day, Purim, and so on.

- Share your own cultural background with the children.

- Talk openly about different races, holidays, and traditions.

- Discuss the positive aspects of differences around the world. Talk about how music, stories, and celebrations sometimes come from different countries and backgrounds.

Strategies to Focus on Self-Esteem

Provide Materials That Build Awareness of Cultural and Ethnic Diversity

Children gain a greater sense of belonging when their heritages are acknowledged and valued. Encourage children to value diversity by providing materials that represent a variety of cultural and ethnic backgrounds. Invite children to bring special items from home as well. Involve parents and other adults who have traveled to other lands (or who may be from other lands) to visit your classroom and share information with the children. Puzzles, manipulatives, dramatic-play area toys, and games from different cultures enable children to see diversity as a natural, enjoyable part of their world. Invite children to draw pictures of what they have learned about a culture different from their own (see journal page on page 51).

"What is special about your background?"

"Have you ever lived in a different country? Do you know someone who has? Tell us about it."

Try Different Foods from Various Cultures

Invite parents or guests from different cultures to come in and give cooking demonstrations. Encourage children in the classroom from different cultures to participate in the demonstrations, if possible. Children then are able to have "tasty treats" and enjoy the foods of other cultures. This helps to build self-esteem for the children because they will have an awareness of the customs and foods of others. This also helps the self-esteem of the children of the specific cultures because others are able to sample a part of their unique heritage.

Read Literature That Expresses Cultural and Ethnic Diversities

Children relate well to stories about heritages and cultures both similar to and different from their own. Encourage children to look at picturebooks about different ethnic backgrounds available in the classroom. Use materials that celebrate diversity for storytimes and as discussion aids. Several books are suggested here for your convenience.

A Promise Is a Promise by Robert Munsch and Michael Kusugak. Altona, Manitoba: D.W. Freisen & Sons, 1988.

Aekyung's Dream by Min Paek. San Francisco: Children's Book Press, 1988.

Angel Child, Dragon Child by Michele Maria Surat and illustrated by Vo-Dinh Mai. Milwaukee: Raintree Publishers, 1983.

Bread Bread Bread by Ann Morris. New York: Lothrop, Lee & Shepard, 1989.

Cornrows by Camille Yarbrough. New York: Coward-McCann Inc., 1979.

Crow Boy by Taro Yashima. New York: Puffin Books, 1976.

Everybody Cooks Rice by Norah Dooley. Minneapolis: Carolrhoda, 1991.

Family Pictures by Carmen Garza as told to Harriet Rohmer. San Francisco: Children's Book Press, 1990.

The Keeping Quilt by Patricia Polacco. New York: Simon & Schuster, 1988.

Lion Dancer: Ernie Wan's Chinese New Year by Kate Waters and Madeline Slovenz-Low. New York: Scholastic, 1990.

Loving by Ann Morris. New York: Lothrop, Lee & Shepard, 1990.

Potato Pancakes All Around: A Hanukkah Tale by Marilyn Hirsh. New York: Bonim Books, 1978.

Star Boy retold and illustrated by Paul Goble. New York: Bradbury Press, 1983.

The Tamarindo Puppy and Other Poems by Charlotte Pomerantz. New York: Greenwillow Books, 1980.

Read Familiar Stories in Different Languages

Several of the stories that children know well are written in other languages. Read "The Three Bears" to the children and then read or invite a Spanish-speaking parent to read "Los Tres Osos." Children will pick up on the words from the other language quickly. Ask the reader to try to use the same inflections for certain parts of the stories. For example, have him or her use the same gruff voice for the father in each of the stories. Or, if there is a child in the classroom who speaks the language that the book is written in, ask him or her to retell the story in that language, if they are not too shy. A youngster from an upper grade who reads or speaks the language can be used as a resource person, too.

Help Children Learn New Words in Two Languages

When there is a child in the classroom whose home language is other than English, involve the parents or guardians of that child in helping to label the things in the classroom—chair, table, pencil, chalk, wall, and so on—in the other language. There can be dual signs signifying acceptance of the other language as valid. While children are learning to read the names in English, they can be learning new words in another language as well!

Name _____

Look What I Have Learned!

Contributing to a Group

Take a Minute...

Children make positive contributions in group settings when they feel secure with themselves. Good self-esteem carries over to working and communicating with others. Think about how each child in your class interacts with others individually and in groups. Consider these options:

- Talk about friends. Ask children how they are helpful to their friends.

- Encourage children to talk about what things they like to do with others.

- Explain to the children that if they choose sometimes to be by themselves, that is okay, too.

Strategies to Focus on Self-Esteem

Discuss Ways Children Are Responsible for Their Actions

When children have responsibilities to others in a group, they feel connected. Talk about making positive choices on the playground, at the drinking fountain, in the hallway, at storytime, and so on. Help children discover that they have choices about their actions. Talk about the variety of positive choices that are available to them in each setting. Then invite children to use the journal page on page 54 to draw pictures of choices they have made, such as playing with a friend, swinging by themselves on the playground, and so on.

"What might you do if someone pushes ahead of you in line?"

"Where might you choose to sit so you can listen carefully at storytime?"

Make Time for Children to Work with Others in Comfortable Settings

Give children opportunities to have positive experiences with others. Assign children buddies for a time period each day. Encourage the assigned buddies to complete at least one classroom activity together before playing with other children. Have assignments at least once a week until the children know one another's names and are able to comfortably interact with several different classmates. Then invite children to draw pictures of themselves doing fun activities with their buddies (see journal page on page 55).

"What activity did you and your buddy do together?"

"What activities are more fun with a friend? What activities are more fun alone?"

Provide Role Models for the Children

Role models can make a difference in the choices young children make. Work with a teacher in an upper grade to develop a buddy system pairing younger children with older students. This not only provides a good role model for the youngsters, but also gives the older students a feeling of accomplishment and value. Set aside a weekly period when the two sets of children can get together. Schedule tutoring periods or physical education periods when the older children can help the younger ones with tasks that are sometimes difficult—hopping, skipping, jumping, or jumping rope. The children can also share a weekly lunch get-together. Older children can also help by taking dictation from the younger children for a story.

Name _____

Name _____

I Like To Do This With My Buddy!

Coping with Loss

Take a Minute...

Coping with loss, whether it is the loss of a pet or someone they love, can be very difficult for children. Children do not understand loss as adults do and don't always know how to ask questions, express their feelings, or deal with their grief. Children are better able to cope with and accept loss as one of life's natural processes when they learn to identify and openly express their feelings. Think about how loss has been dealt with in the past in your classroom. Consider these options:

- Talk about loss openly in the classroom.

- Give children ample time to talk and grieve, whether with the class or alone, if necessary.

- Keep communication open with the family when a child is grieving.

Strategies to Focus on Self-Esteem

Accept Children's Feelings About Loss

Being able to share feelings openly helps children identify and feel okay about their needs during an experience of loss. Encourage the children to openly discuss their feelings about a loss—a friend who has moved, a classroom pet that has died, a grandparent who has passed away, and so on. Help children focus on their positive memories. Invite the children to make "Happy Memory" books illustrating fun moments they have experienced in the past with the person, pet, or other perceived loss (see journal page on page 57).

Read Literature That Expresses Loss in Appropriate Ways for the Children

There are many good books that help children identify their emotions. Provide opportunities for children to discuss the emotions that the books, like the four suggested here, address.

Annie and the Old One by Miska Miles. Boston: Little, Brown and Company, 1971.

My Grandson Lew by Charlotte Zolotow. New York: Harper & Row, 1974.

Nana Upstairs and Nana Downstairs by Tomie de Paola. New York: Putnam, 1987.

The Tenth Good Thing About Barney by Judith Viorst. New York: Atheneum, 1971.

Name _____

My Happy Memory About...

Learning to Communicate

Take a Minute...

Learning good communication skills helps children develop good relationships with others. Think about the children in your classroom and each child's way of communicating with others. Consider these options:

- Make sure each child has enough time for "show and tell." Time to talk about themselves is important.

- Consider how often children communicate with each other. Are certain children withdrawn? Encourage cooperative-learning time where each child can participate.

Your nonverbal language can be a strong indicator of how you feel about someone or something. Children are very quick to pick up on nonverbal language.

If a child behaves in a way you disapprove of, it may be a way of getting your attention. These are the children who need to have their self-worth built up the most. These children will bloom and most likely stop the inappropriate behavior as you continue to work with them.

Something else to keep in mind: When children are showing something to the class or doing a language-development lesson, make sure you give them your full attention. Children need the strokes that come from a teacher's questions and interest.

Strategies to Focus on Self-Esteem

Point Out Ways That Nonverbal Language May Be Used to Communicate

Understanding different forms of communication helps children more effectively communicate with and relate to others. Ask children to show you how they feel about things without using words: spinach, ice cream, puppies, chores, bedtime, parties, and so on. Discuss ways that children and adults "talk" to one another without using words. You may want to introduce sign language as another way to communicate without spoken words. Invite children to draw nonverbal feelings on the journal page provided on page 61. Share the pictures with the class and see if they can guess what emotion is being expressed in each one.

"When might it be helpful to use your body to show your feelings rather than words? When is it not helpful?"

Provide Opportunities for Children to Learn Other Languages

Invite a classmate (or classroom guest) who speaks another language to teach the children some words. Or, ask the visitor to teach the children to count or sing a song. Teach children several common words in other languages. Then encourage the children to use the words throughout the day. The children may enjoy learning more about the countries where these languages are spoken as well.

Spanish	French	Swahili	English
uno	un	moja	one
dos	deux	mbili	two
tres	trois	atu	three
cuatro	quatre	nne	four
cinco	cinq	tano	five
seis	six	sita	six
siete	sept	saba	seven
ocho	huit	nane	eight
nueve	neuf	tisa	nine
diez	dix	kumi	ten

Discuss Other Ways to Communicate

If differences among children are recognized, accepted, and treated as a positive influence in the classroom environment and curriculum, those children who use sing language, Braille, or speak another language will feel more comfortable. Young children can learn very quickly how to sign. They can learn the alphabet and then learn songs or fingerplays in sign language as well. Children can also be introduced to Braille. Ask a person who reads Braille to come in and show the children how Braille is read by someone who uses it.

Hold a Signing Presentation

Arrange for the children to sing a song and then sign a song at an open house or other school presentation. Parents then become aware of the diversity of the classrooms, the acceptance of the children, and the building of self-esteem for those children who do speak another language.

Provide Opportunities for Children to Learn Songs in Other Languages

A parent or friend who speaks a language other than English can be invited to the classroom to teach a song in that language. There are recorded songs available to use if a speaker is not available. If a child is not shy about using the home language, that child can be appointed as song leader.

Help Children to Create Their Own Ways to Communicate

Invite the children to make up their own way of communicating. Ask children to think of a new way to say "Hello," "Goodbye," "I Like You," and so on, using nonverbal language. Then encourage the children to draw pictures of their new ways to communicate (see journal page on page 62)!

Name _____

Look At Me! How Am I Feeling?

Name _____

This Is How I Say . . .

Reflections:

How I Help Children Connect in My Classroom

❑ I provide materials that express cultural and ethnic diversity.

❑ I make sure that my classroom is open to discussion and questions about different cultures, backgrounds, and ways of life.

❑ I encourage children to openly discuss their feelings about loss.

❑ I provide opportunities for children to talk about their families and the role each child plays within his or her family.

❑ I make picturebooks available in my classroom about different family structures and situations.

❑ I help children talk about their families and express their emotions.

❑ I provide consistency for the children in discipline, direction, and promises.

❑ I provide opportunities for children to make choices. I reinforce the positive choices children make.

❑ I use the buddy system in my classroom.

❏ I make children aware of the impact of nonverbal communication.

❏ I care about children's needs. I listen to the concerns of the children. In this way, I am able to gain their trust.

❏ I help the children understand that it is important that they are trusted.

❏ I am aware of how nonverbal language affects the children.

❏ I provide opportunities for children to learn words in other languages.

I Like Who I Am & It Shows © 1993 Fearon Teacher Aids

I Am Capable

A child with a low opinion of his or her capabilities may try to control other people or things. On the other hand, a child who feels that he or she has positive capabilities will more easily accept realistic limitations, knowing he or she can accomplish his or her goals despite limitations. A sense of one's own capabilities determines how children use their capabilities and how they feel about what they do.

Building Blocks Strategies Included in This Unit

- ❤ Cooperating with Others
- ❤ Following Rules
- ❤ Handling Criticism
- ❤ Helping Others
- ❤ Making Choices
- ❤ Taking Risks
- ❤ Rewards

Cooperating with Others

Take a Minute...

Knowing with reassurance what will come next can be important to youngsters, especially those who are at risk because of various outside forces. The security of the classroom is, at times, the only structure available to some unfortunate children. When children are given responsibilities and feel important to the structure of the class, they are then able to use these skills to contribute to a group and cooperate with others. Think about the group goals achieved in your classroom. Do you ask the children to help with tasks? Consider these options:

- Ask children to help set up snacktime or the dramatic-play area—include small tasks for each child.

- At the end of the day, ask children to help straighten up the classroom by giving each child a small task—picking up blocks, pushing in chairs, hanging up clothes, and so on—so the clean-up job can be done cooperatively.

- Talk to parents and guardians about goal-setting at home. Discuss how sometimes too much is expected of children which may lead to discouragement because of failure. Suggest that chores at home be given out in small increments and not all at once, such as picking up toys, helping care for siblings, hanging up or folding clothes, straightening bedding, helping set the table, or clearing the dishes.

Strategies to Focus on Self-Esteem

Enlist Children's Help to Complete Tasks That Clearly Require More Than One Person

Help the children make a list of the tasks they can do alone—with two hands. Point out that even though it feels great to be able to do things on one's own, there are some tasks that either require more than two hands, or that are just more fun if more than one person participates. Encourage the children to name some of these tasks—games, class projects, classroom jobs, and so on. Then provide opportunities for children to participate in these types of group projects. Invite children to draw pictures of their shared tasks on the journal page on page 68.

"What jobs need more than one person to do them?"

"How would it help to have two people do a job rather than just one person?"

Help Children with Goal-Setting

Start each day by verbalizing your own goals for the day. Then explain to the children your class goals for the first hour of the day. Encourage the children to share how they might help achieve these goals. At the end of the hour, discuss the results—what worked well, what might be improved upon, and so on. When the children feel comfortable about the order of activities for the first hour, add another hour to the discussion. Then invite children to use the journal page on page 69 to illustrate how they can help achieve a classroom goal!

"How can you help with _____ today?"

Discuss How Sharing Helps Us Work Together

Show children that sharing and including others leads to cooperation with everyone. When cooperating with others, children need to learn to play together nicely, share, and include others in their play and work time. Learning this at an early age helps the self-esteem of all children. When children are valued by their peers, it reaffirms their own self-worth.

Name _____

I Need A Friend To Help Me Do This...

I Like Who I Am & It Shows © 1993 Fearon Teacher Aids

Name _____

Following Rules

Take a Minute...

Children feel in control of their environment when rules and limits are clear and they understand the consequences of their actions. Think about what rules you currently have in your classroom. Do you spend time going over rules with the children? Consider these options:

- Talk about classroom rules often. Ask the children to tell you what the rules are periodically.

- Invite the children to share in rule-making, if possible. For example, children can help with the rules for snacktime, game rules, playground rules, and so on. Involve families in the class rule-making as well.

- At back-to-school night or at the first opportunity to talk to parents or guardians, class rules can be explained in a friendly environment. Parents then will be aware of what the expectations are, both for the children and for the teacher.

Strategies to Focus on Self-Esteem

Have Children Restate Classroom Rules to Be Certain They Understand Them

Some children who we assume are deliberately disobeying rules have instead misinterpreted them. A good introduction to the establishment of rules in the classroom is the book *Miss Nelson Is Missing* (see the bibliography on page 92). Read the story to the children and then invite children to help make up some rules for your classroom. Post the rules in the classroom as a friendly reminder. To make sure that all children understand the rules, follow the procedure outlined here. When a child breaks a rule, ask the child to state his or her interpretation of the rule and his or her understanding of the consequence. Then follow through as appropriate.

- Clarify the agreed-upon rules for the children.

- Have the children restate the rules in their own words.

- Ask children to follow the rules.

Invite children to draw pictures of their most important rule (see journal page on page 72)!

Help Children Understand the Natural Consequences of Their Behavior

The difference between natural consequences and punishment lies primarily in the placement of power. Punishment gives the teacher sole control and implies that children are bad, rather than that their behaviors are wrong. Consequences spring naturally from situations—this message affirms that the behavior is wrong, not that the child is bad.

> "You forgot your boots. You'll need to play on the blacktop today. But if you remember to bring your boots tomorrow, you can play in the snow!"

Name _____

Handling Criticism

Take a Minute...

Even adults sometimes have a hard time handling criticism. If we, as teachers, encourage children to focus on their abilities and the positive aspects of themselves, criticism will seem less devastating to them. Stressing the good things about a child rather than the bad helps children focus on what they are capable of and their self-esteem increases. Think about the types of criticism you use in your classroom—negative or positive? Consider these options:

- Have the children brainstorm all of the positive words that they can think of. Then each child can be assigned a good word that he or she can use at least once during the day when addressing another member of the class.

- Suggest to the children that they play the game at home, too. Ask children to use the "good word" when talking to a guardian, parent, or sibling. If the children use the word casually in conversation at home, there may be some carryover to other family members.

Strategies to Focus on Self-Esteem

Free Children from Labels

Children tend to behave in ways they perceive they are viewed by others. By the time children enter school, they sometimes have set images of themselves—slow, clumsy, irresponsible, smart, creative, and so on. Other children will quickly pick up on the roles and respond to them. Look for opportunities to help children who see themselves negatively to see themselves in new, more positive ways. For example, when a child is labeled "forgetful," verify those times when the child remembers. Invite children to draw pictures of something they can do well (see journal page on page 75)! Talk about the pictures with the children.

> "With everything else you've had to do today, you remembered to put the paintbrushes away. That's very responsible!"

Give Children Opportunities to Avoid Labeling

Name-calling will diminish when children see their classmates in positive ways. A child who is viewed as greedy by his or her peers might be asked to pass out pencils evenly to his or her classmates. A child who is often disorganized might be given responsibilites that guarantee success and also bolster self-esteem.

"Can you help me get five cartons of milk for snacktime?"

"Which would you rather do first, bring out the snacks
  or pour the juice?"

Name _____

Look What I Can Do!

Helping Others

Take a Minute...

Children feel more able to help others when they feel good about themselves. By helping someone else, self-esteem continues to grow because we are helping others with their self-esteem as well. Think about how the children in your classroom help others. Is help freely given? Consider these options:

- Talk about how children can help others in the classroom.

- Ask children to share about times they have helped others, as well as times someone has helped them. Ask children how they feel when they help others.

Strategies to Focus on Self-Esteem

Set a Good Example of Helping Others

Children are more likely to learn to care for others if you model a helping role for them. Share with the children the good deeds you do to help others. Identify the good feelings you experience when you help others as well. Encourage children to look for opportunities to help others in the classroom. Set up a "good deeds" bulletin board in the classroom. Invite the children (including yourself) to contribute records of the good deeds they and others do each day. Then invite children to draw pictures of how they helped someone at home (see journal page on page 78).

"I helped my sister do the dishes. How can you help your brother, sister, or someone else at home today?"

Teach Children the Joy That Comes from Giving Without Others Knowing!

Children love to play tricks on one another. How about doing nice things for others without getting caught! Help the children make a list of tasks that they might do to help others. Then challenge the children to do one or more of the tasks for members of their family or for their classmates during the week—without getting caught! At the end of the week, invite the children to share their feelings about this activity. This can be a fun game that rewards both the giver and receiver with warm feelings. Self-esteem among class members will almost certainly be enhanced as well.

"How do you feel when you do something nice for someone else?"

Discuss Role Models with the Children

Discuss with children people they know that have helped others, such as people who serve food to the poor. Ask the children to think of others to add to the list as well.

Name _____

I'm So Proud! Look How I Helped!

I Like Who I Am & It Shows © 1993 Fearon Teacher Aids

Making Choices

Take a Minute...

Children feel more responsible when they have opportunities to make choices. By providing children with choices, they feel more capable and important. Think about the choices offered in your classroom. Consider these options:

- Be aware of children who have problems making choices. Help them learn to make choices they can feel proud of.

- Invite children to take part in choices in the classroom, such as what book to read at storytime, where to go on an outing, and so on.

Strategies to Focus on Self-Esteem

Help Children Express Their Feelings, Recognize They Have Choices, and Realize That Every Choice Has a Consequence

It is unreasonable to expect young children to control their feelings and impulses. However, we can and should teach children the consequences of impulsive actions. If a child is angry and starts throwing things, help the child verbalize why he or she is angry. Offer alternatives to throwing, such as telling you how he or she feels. This helps children understand that they can choose to react differently. The first step is to gently help the young child evaluate a past behavior.

"What were you feeling? What did you do? Then what happened?"

Help children use the journal page on page 80 to help them understand and verbalize their feelings. Help them draw pictures of why they feel the way they do and what happened.

Provide Opportunities for Children to Make Choices

Disciplining a child may leave that child feeling bad or with hurt feelings. By giving a child a choice in a situation, he or she will be part of the learning process and has an opportunity to feel good about his or her appropriate choices.

"Which would you rather share? Your red crayon or your blue crayon?"

"Would you like to help Mary pick up the blocks now or before recess?"

"Will you use a rag or paper towels to wipe up the spill?"

Name _____

I Like Who I Am & It Shows © 1993 Fearon Teacher Aids

Taking Risks

Take a Minute...

Children are more likely to take risks when they feel good about themselves. Fear is a normal part of the learning process. Help children try new things by starting with small risks—their success with the small risk will build their self-confidence. Children will then have less fear of failure and begin to feel better about taking other appropriate risks as well. Think about how children take risks in your classroom. Consider these options:

- Talk to the children about the things they are afraid of trying. By talking about these things, fears diminish.

- Some children have more fear than others. Start less confident children with smaller risks.

- Talk to children about new things they would like to try. Encourage children to use their imaginations. Then invite the children to draw pictures of the new things they want to try (see journal page on page 83).

Strategies to Focus on Self-Esteem

Be Accepting of Children's Feelings of Fear

Help children identify the sources of their feelings of fear. Typically, young children are afraid of ghosts and other imagined creatures. Invite the children to help make a list of some of the things they are afraid of— real and imagined. Then provide opportunities for the children to use dramatic-play or drawing and painting to recreate their scary feelings and experiences so that they may more easily identify and overcome their feelings.

Talk About Fears the Children Have Conquered

Ask the children if they have ever been afraid of something that they are not afraid of anymore. Then ask the children how they felt once they weren't afraid any longer. Encourage discussion. Talking about past fears helps children see that they can get past some of the fears they have now. Then have children draw pictures of things they used to be afraid of when they were little, but aren't afraid of anymore (see journal page on page 84).

Provide Opportunities for Children to Practice Solving Problems

Children's fears diminish when they see that they have some control over what happens around them. Encourage children to think of things they could do in scary situations. Invite children to be creative! For example, what would they do if a large, scary-looking dog approached them, they had to have a shot at the doctor's office, and so on? Encourage the children to suggest many different responses for each situation. Then invite children to draw pictures of themselves responding to a scary situation (see journal page on page 85).

Name _____

I'd Like To Try This...

Name _____

When I Was Little, I Was Afraid Of...

Name _____

This Is What I'd Do... If I Were Scared!

Rewards

Take a Minute...

Children need rewards that acknowledge their good work. Think about the reward system in your classroom. It is important that all children be rewarded for something over a period of time. Children are keenly aware of being left out. Consider these options:

- Ask children to suggest specific rewards for certain things, such as going on an outing after a project is finished or singing a special song after the classroom has been straightened up.

- Have an awards day and award each child with a special reward—best chalkboard eraser, greatest lost-notebook finder, best snacktime helper, and so on.

Strategies to Focus on Self-Esteem

Establish a Reward System in Your Classroom

Children can receive rewards for good work, good behavior, or following the rules. One of the nicest rewards, good for both children and parents or guardians, is a note home or a telephone call to acknowledge the good behavior. Parents are very quick to hear about any misbehavior—a reward system should inform parents about the positive, too.

Provide Rewards for Group Activities

Involve all of the children in book-writing efforts, science projects, or art fairs. Explain to the children that there are no losers when everyone has done his or her best to put together a book, science exhibit, or art activity. Everyone gets a ribbon as a "participant."

Reflections:

How I Help Children Feel Capable in My Classroom

❑ I take time at the beginning of each day to discuss class goals.

❑ I involve the children in meaningful group work—work that clearly requires more than one person to complete.

❑ When children disobey rules, I first check to see if they understood the rules.

❑ The rules in my classroom have natural consequences if they are broken.

❑ I try to compliment each child in my classroom at least once a day.

❑ I provide opportunities for children to see themselves in positive roles.

❑ I set a good example of helping others for the children. I share with them the good deeds I do and encourage them to do the same.

❑ I enlist the children's help in setting safety rules and sharing in the responsibility of following these rules.

❑ I encourage children to express their feelings by helping them evaluate their past behaviors.

❑ The children are provided with many experiences to make choices.

❑ When disciplining children, I try to provide them with choices.

❑ I encourage children to talk about their fears. Then we work together to create strategies for helping them deal with their fears.

❑ I encourage the children to try new things.

I Like Who I Am & It Shows © 1993 Fearon Teacher Aids

The Next Step

We cannot begin to help children focus on their possibilities
unless we do the same for ourselves.

❑ End each day by listing all the
good things you have
accomplished—no matter how
small they may seem.

❑ Think of how helping children
have good self-esteem is positive
for your classroom.

❑ Each night, think of what you can
accomplish tomorrow as a result of
what you learned during the day.

Bibliography

The following books are resources that will be helpful as you work
to improve young children's self-esteem. Enjoy the books during storytimes with
the class or offer the books in library corners for children to enjoy individually.
You may wish to make copies of this bibliography to share with parents.

Abiyoyo by Pete Seeger. New York: Macmillan, 1986.
A magician and his son go from outcasts to heroes when they
vanquish a monster who has been terrorizing their village.
A story-song with music included. Ages 5-8.

Alfie Gets in First by Shirley Hughes. New York: Lothrop,
Lee & Shepard Books, 1982.
When Alfie rushes into the house before his mother and slams the
door, he finds himself in big trouble. Then he finds a way to reach the
lock! Ages 3-5.

All by Myself by Anna Grossnickle Hines. New York: Clarion, 1984.
One night Josie gets to the bathroom in the dark—all by herself!
Ages 3-5.

Arthur's Prize Reader by Lillian Hoban. New York: Harper & Row, 1978.
Big brother Arthur becomes a reading teacher when he helps his
younger sister figure out the hard words as well as the easy ones.
Little Violet proves the more perceptive reader in this funny easy-
to-read story of chimpanzee siblings. Ages 6-8.

The Big Orange Splot by Daniel Manus Pinkwater. Mamaroneck,
NY: Hastings House, 1977.
Mr. Plumbean and his neighbors were content being just alike.
By accident one day they discover how happy they are when
showing their individuality. Ages 4-7.

Bodies by Barbara Brenner. New York: E. P. Dutton, 1973.
A picturebook of bodies—every size, shape, color, sex, and age—with
a simple text that praises the uniqueness of each individual. Ages 3-5.

Brown Bear, Brown Bear, What Do You See? by Bill Martin, Jr. New York:
Holt, 1983.
Eric Carle's strongly colored collages of animals are asked what
animals they see. The answers follow. Young children gain a sense
of accomplishment as they develop prediction skills. Older children
may create their own "Brown Bear" rhymes. Ages 1 and up.

Chin Chiang and the Dragon's Dance by Ian Wallace. New York: Margaret K. McElderry Books, 1984.
Chin Chiang masters the steps of the dragon's dance in time to join his grandfather in the Chinese New Year celebration. Ages 5-8.

Clive Eats Alligators by Alison Lester. Boston: Houghton Mifflin, 1986.
Seven children wear different clothes, play different games, eat different snacks, and take naps in different places. Each child is special in the activities that make up his or her day. Ages 3-5.

Crow Boy by Taro Yashima. New York: Viking Press, 1955.
A solitary boy, with the help of a kind teacher, gains the admiration of his classmates. Ages 5-8.

Flossie and the Fox by Patricia McKissack. New York: Dial, 1986.
Young Flossie uses her wits to triumph over a greedy fox in this tale from the black tradition of the rural South. Ages 4-7.

Frederick by Leo Lionni. New York: Pantheon, 1967.
While the other mice gather food for the winter, Frederick gathers words, which he puts into poems that warm and cheer his friends when winter comes. Ages 4-7.

Frosted Glass by Denys Cazet. New York: Bradbury, 1987.
Gregory is a dog whose imaginative drawings don't meet the requirements of class assignments. When Gregory's teacher recognizes his creativity, Gregory realizes that his work has value. Ages 5-8.

The Goat in the Rug by Charles Blood. New York: Macmillan, 1980.
Just as every Navajo weaver has done for hundreds of years, Glenmae, with the help of her goat, Geraldine, creates a rug design that can never be duplicated. Ages 5-8.

How My Parents Learned to Eat by Ina Friedman. Boston: Houghton Mifflin, 1984.
A young daughter tells how her father, an American sailor, and her mother, a Japanese school girl, secretly learned each other's ways of eating before going out on a dinner date. Ages 5-8.

I Can Do It by Myself by Lessie J. Little. New York: T.Y. Crowell Co., 1978.
A fierce bulldog is the main obstacle Donnie faces after he shops successfully for his mother's birthday present. Despite crying and falling down, Donnie makes it home with his sense of pride and accomplishment intact. Ages 3-5.

I Like Me by Nancy Carlson. New York: Viking Press, 1988.
By showing that she can take care of herself and have fun when there is no one else around, a young pig proves the best friend you can have is yourself. Ages 3-5.

I Speak English for My Mom by Muriel Stanek. Niles, IL: Albert Whitman & Co., 1988.
> Because her mother only speaks and reads Spanish, Lupe Gomez must help her mother shop, go to the dentist, and more— even though Lupe would rather be playing. Ages 5-8.

Imogene's Antlers by David Small. New York: Crown, 1985.
> Imogene handles the appearance of antlers growing out of her head with cheerful aplomb. She then finds a way to put the unwanted encumbrance to work for her. Ages 4-7.

The Josefina Story Quilt by Eleanor Coerr. New York: Harper & Row, 1986.
> In this easy-to-read pioneer story, Faith quilts a patchwork story of her heroic hen, Josefina. Ages 5-8.

King Bidgood's in the Bathtub by Audrey Wood. San Diego: Harcourt Brace Jovanovich, 1985.
> A young page succeeds in forcing the king out of the bathtub after efforts by the queen, the duke, and others fail. Ages 3-5.

The Ladder in the Sky retold by Barbara Jan Esbensen. Boston: Little, Brown and Company, 1989.
> This Ojibway legend, illustrated with detailed paintings, tells how the Ojibway learned to heal themselves. Ages 7 and up.

Little Gorilla by Ruth Bornstein. New York: Clarion, 1976.
> As a baby and toddler, Little Gorilla is adored by all the animals in the forest. Then he starts to grow and grow—and doubts whether he is still lovable in his large form. Ages 2-4.

Lizzie's Invitation by Holly Keller. New York: Greenwillow Books, 1987.
> Lizzie and her new friend, Amanda, create their own good time when neither is invited to a classmate's party. Ages 5-8.

Miss Nelson Is Missing by Harry Allard. Boston: Houghton Mifflin, 1984.
> The nicest teacher in the school is missing and her misbehaving students have a new teacher—the witch-like Miss Swamp. Miss Nelson comes back to a better behaved class, but only Miss Nelson and the readers know where she has been! Ages 5-8.

Miss Rumphius by Barbara Cooney. New York: Viking Press, 1982.
> Alice Rumphius fulfills a childhood promise made to her grandfather that she will make the world more beautiful. Ages 5-8.

My Friend Jacob by Lucille Clifton. New York: E. P. Dutton, 1980.
> Sam is eight and his friend, Jacob, who is mentally handicapped, is seventeen. Sam describes how he and Jacob help each other and share Jacob's triumphs, which include learning to knock on a door. Ages 5-8.

I Like Who I Am & It Shows © 1993 Fearon Teacher Aids

My Mother the Mail Carrier—Mi Mama La Cartera by Inez Maury. Old Westbury, NY: Feminist Press, 1976.

Lupita's mother is strong, brave, and a good cook. She loves outings and likes her work. But Lupita wants to be a jockey when she grows up. This is a well-designed bilingual book. Ages 5-8.

Nobody's Perfect, Not Even My Mother by Norma Simon. Niles, IL: Albert Whitman & Co., 1981.

One child is good at puzzles and another is good at photography. A mother is a good mechanic and a father is a good bricklayer. This is a light approach to helping children understand that everyone excels in some things, but nobody is perfect. Ages 4-7.

Peek-a-BOO! by Janet and Allan Ahlberg. New York: Penguin Press, 1981.

This is a book that will fascinate children for years as they peek through small circles on pages to see detailed pictures of Baby in complex and active scenes. Ages 2-5.

People by Peter Spier. New York: Doubleday, 1980.

This wordless book delightfully illustrates the uniqueness and diversity of people. Ages 4-8.

Pulgada a Pulgada (Inch by Inch) by Leo Lionni. New York: Astor-Honor, 1961.

A lowly inchworm proves his worth to haughty birds and to himself. Ages 4-7.

Shawn Goes to School by Petronella Breinburg. New York: Harper & Row, 1973.

Shawn overcomes his fear of nursery school when he discovers "lots of nice kids" swinging and a donkey to ride. Ages 4-6.

Shy Charles by Rosemary Wells. New York: Dial, 1987.

Even after proving himself a hero, Charles remains in character—shy! Ages 4-7.

Sing a Song of Popcorn: Every Child's Book of Poems selected by Beatrice Schenk de Regniers. New York: Scholastic, 1988.

Share the 128 poems divided into nine thematic sections. Cultural diversity is represented in the subject matter by famous poets and popular artists. Ages 5-10.

So What by Miriam Cohen. New York: Greenwillow Books, 1982.

Jim can't master the monkey bars, his club fails, and he's the shortest child in the first grade. It takes Elinor's words, "so what," to help Jim understand that his concerns are trivial before he is free to succeed at something. Ages 4-7.

Someone Special, Just Like You by Tricia Brown. New York: Holt, 1984.
Black-and-white photographs show preschool children with physical, mental, and sensory disabilities playing and learning. The brief text shows that it is not children's differences, but their similarities, that make all children special. Ages 4-6.

Toad Is the Uncle of Heaven: A Vietnamese Folk Tale retold by Jeanne M. Lee. New York: Holt, 1985.
Lowly Toad uses his wits and courage to save the Earth from a scorching drought. To this day, in Vietnam, the toad is a symbol of rain. Ages 5-8.

Troll Country by Edward Marshall. New York: Dial, 1980.
Elsie finds a new way to trick a green, smelly troll she meets in the deep, dark forest. Ages 5-8.

Umbrella by Taro Yashima. New York: Penguin, 1958.
Momo longs for a rainy day so she can use the red umbrella she received on her third birthday. When that day arrives, Momo is so proud of her umbrella that she walks alone, without holding her parents' hands. Ages 3-5.

The Wednesday Surprise by Eve Bunting. New York: Clarion, 1989.
Anna and her grandma work in secret on a present for dad's birthday that only they can give him! Ages 5-8.

Whistle for Willie by Ezra Jack Keats. New York: Penguin, 1964.
Peter has a reason to learn to whistle. Success is his in a small boy's urban adventure. Ages 4-7.

Wilfrid Gordon McDonald Partridge by Mem Fox. New York: Kane/Miller, 1985.
A small boy helps his 96-year-old neighbor recover her "lost memory." Ages 4-7.

Notes